A STAR IN A MARMALADE JAR

By Cynthia Rider

Illustrated by Sarah Warburton

CAMBRIDGE
UNIVERSITY PRESS

On Monday morning,
Charlie Smart
went to the market
with his horse and cart.
He saw a shining silver star,
a silver star in a marmalade jar.

2

"I'd like that star,"
said Charlie Smart.
"Here is my money
and my good farm cart."

3

Back to his farm went Charlie Smart,
without his money and without his cart.
Without the food and without the hay
that he should have got in town that day.

4

But Charlie Smart had a silver star,
a silver star in a marmalade jar.

5

He showed the star to his wife, Ann.
She said, "You *are* a silly man.
Why did you buy a star today?
What we need is food and hay.

The barns are empty.
The larder is bare.
Oh, Charlie, Charlie, don't you care?
The grass won't grow
and the hen won't lay,
and now you've given our cart away!"

7

Charlie said, "But don't you see,
I want to set this poor star free.
It isn't right to keep a star
inside an empty marmalade jar."

8

Ann said, "Yes, I must agree.
This silver star should be set free."

9

So when it was dark,
they opened the jar,
and into the sky
went the sparkling star.

10

Then silver stardust
fell on the farm.
It fell on the garden
and onto the barn.

11

The very next day
their little hen, Meg,
laid a shining, silver egg.
The big farm cat
ran around the house,
after a smart little silver mouse.

12

They saw that the cow
had silver horns.
The dogs had silver paws,
and all the barn rats said,
"What fun!
We've all got silver claws."

13

Ann's larder now was full of food.
The barns were full of hay.
"Just look," said Ann.
"Just look," said Charlie.
"It must be our lucky day."

14

Then, as it started to get dark,
the two farm dogs began to bark.
There in the farmyard, Charlie Smart
saw a brand-new silver cart!

15

"What a perfect end
to a perfect day,"
said Charlie with a sigh.
Then far up in the dark night sky,
Charlie and Ann saw a star.
"The silver star did this," they said.
"The star from the marmalade jar!"

16